595

621

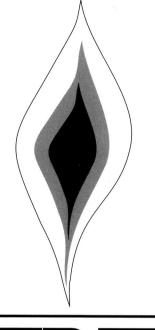

POWER FROM THE WIND

Hazel Songhurst

Wayland

Other titles in this series include:
Power from the Earth
Power from Plants
Power from the Sun
Power from Water

Cover: A wind farm in California in the USA.

Designer: David Armitage

Text is based on *Wind Energy* in the *Alternative Energy* series published in 1990.

Picture acknowledgements
Biofotos 23 (Heather Angel); David Bowden 5 (left), 17 (right); British Aeropsace/Wind Energy Group 16, 19 (both), 20; Danish Wind Energy Association 24; Energy Technology Support Unit 26 (right); Environmental Picture Library cover (Rob Franklin); Eye Ubiquitous 8, 13, 26 (left); Greenpeace 4, 5 (right); Japan Ship Centre 25; Christine Osborne 10, 12; Topham Picture Library 9, 11; United States Department of Energy 17 (left), 18, 21. All artwork is by Nick Hawken.

First published in 1993 by
Wayland (Publishers) Limited

British Library Cataloguing in Publication Data
Songhurst, Hazel
Power from the Wind. - (Energy series)
I. Title II. Series
333.9
ISBN 0 7502 0812 0

Typeset by Perspective Marketing Limited

Printed in Italy by G. Canale & C.S.p.A.

Contents

Making electricity

For a long time, electricity has been made by burning coal, oil and gas. These are called fossil fuels.

Fossil fuels are starting to run out. They have also caused damage to the environment. Today, scientists are looking at new, safer ways to make the power we need.

Fossil fuels give off poisonous gases when they are burned.

The banner on this chimney says 'Stop acid rain'. Acid rain is a very poisonous type of pollution. It is caused by burning coal.

These windsurfers are using the power of the wind to move across the water. In the future, wind power can be used to make electricity.

Energy from the wind

Winds are moving air. They are formed when the heat from the Sun warms up cool air near the ground. The warmed-up air rises, and cool air rushes in to take its place.

The diagram below shows how winds are formed.

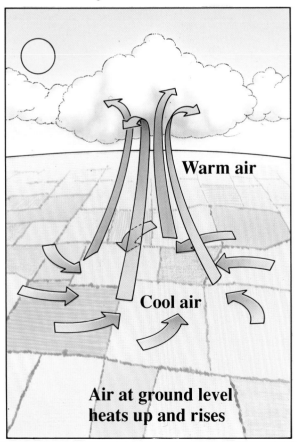

Warm air

Cool air

Air at ground level heats up and rises

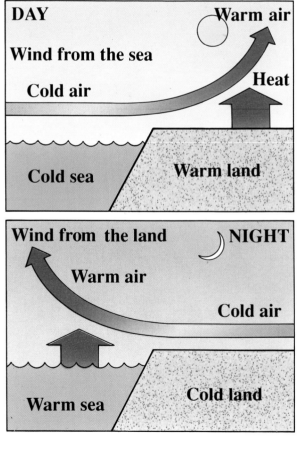

DAY

Warm air

Wind from the sea

Cold air

Heat

Cold sea

Warm land

Wind from the land

NIGHT

Warm air

Cold air

Warm sea

Cold land

Winds also form at coasts.

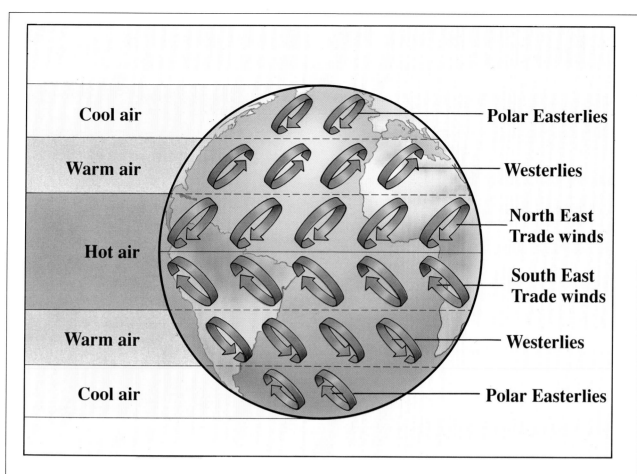

Cool air	Polar Easterlies
Warm air	Westerlies
Hot air	North East Trade winds
	South East Trade winds
Warm air	Westerlies
Cool air	Polar Easterlies

These are the winds that blow over the world all the time. The Sun warms the air more in some parts of the world than in others.

The faster the air moves from one place to another, the stronger the wind. The strongest winds of all are called hurricanes.

This machine is an anemometer. It works out how fast the wind is blowing. The cups on top spin round and the wind's speed is shown on the scale.

Wind contains large amounts of kinetic (moving) energy. If this energy is trapped it can be used to make electricity.

Wind energy alone cannot make all the power we need. This is because winds are always changing and do not give out the same amount of energy all the time. But in the future, as much as one-fifth of all our electricity could come from the wind.

The power of a hurricane wrecked this man's home in Texas, USA.

Early wind power

The power of the wind was first used about 5,000 years ago when people began to make sails for boats. When the wind filled the sail it pushed the boat along.

These sailing boats from Abu Dhabi are like the boats people sailed thousands of years ago.

Can you count how many sails there are on this old clipper sailing ship? Two hundred years ago, clippers were the fastest ships on the oceans.

This drawing shows you how the first windmills worked. This windmill was used in Persia (now called Iran) about 2,000 years ago.

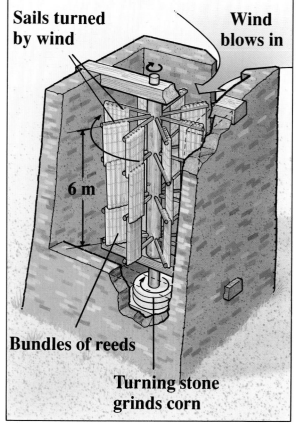

Sails turned by wind

Wind blows in

6 m

Bundles of reeds

Turning stone grinds corn

This old Greek windmill has sails just like the sails on a boat. Can you see they are filled with wind?

For hundreds of years, windmills were used to grind corn. When steam and diesel engines were invented, windmills were no longer used.

This post mill in the Netherlands is still used today for sawing wood. Post mills can also be used for pumping water and making paper.

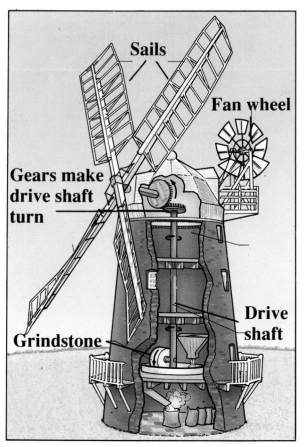

Sails

Fan wheel

Gears make drive shaft turn

Grindstone

Drive shaft

This diagram shows how a tower mill works. Can you see the fan wheel at the back? It turns the sails to face into the wind.

Wind power today

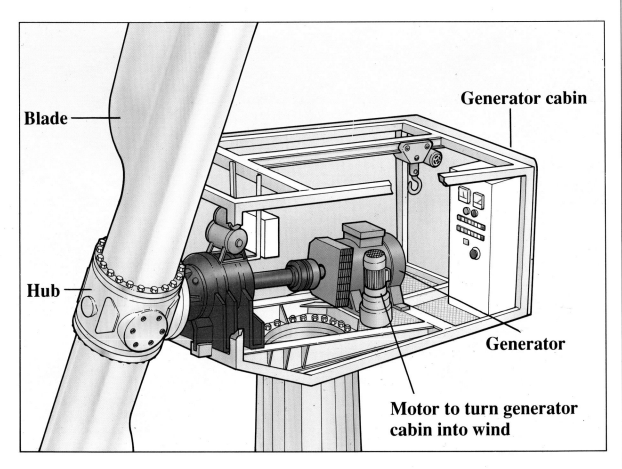

Blade

Generator cabin

Hub

Generator

Motor to turn generator cabin into wind

This diagram shows the inside of a wind turbine. The wind turns the blades. These drive the generator to make electricity.

Wind turbines are modern wind machines that make electricity. Like the old windmills, they use the energy of the wind to turn machinery.

There are many different kinds of wind turbines. They are divided into two main types - horizontal axis and vertical axis.

Horizontal axis turbines have blades that spin round a lengthways axis. Vertical axis turbines have blades that spin round an upright axis.

Different kinds of wind turbines.

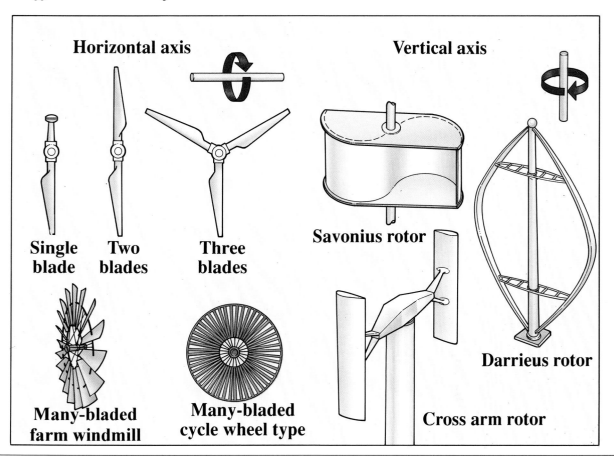

Horizontal axis

Vertical axis

Single blade **Two blades** **Three blades**

Savonius rotor

Many-bladed farm windmill **Many-bladed cycle wheel type** **Cross arm rotor** **Darrieus rotor**

The enormous blades of a wind turbine being tested for strength.

The blades on a wind turbine are curved like aeroplane wings. They are made of light, very strong material. Whenever the wind changes, the blades move to face into it. In strong winds, brakes slow them down.

This windpump in the USA pumps up water from the river. The water is sprayed on crops.

The photograph on the left shows a Darrieus turbine being tested in California, USA. It has two thin, curved metal blades which spin round its axis.

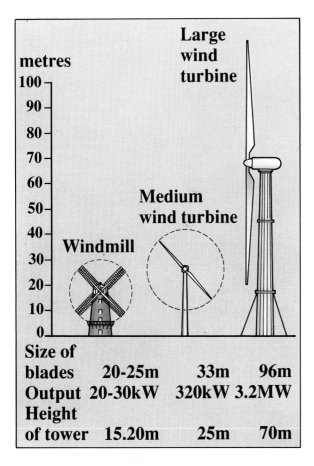

Size of blades	20-25m	33m	96m
Output	20-30kW	320kW	3.2MW
Height of tower	15.20m	25m	70m

This chart looks at how much electricity different types of wind machines can make.

It is easy to see that the bigger the machine, the more powerful it is.

This tall wind turbine is in California, USA. Its height and long blades allow it to make more electricity than a smaller turbine.

The biggest turbines can make more than
1 megawatt (MW) of electric power. That
is enough power to light up 10,000
lightbulbs all at once.

These are two of the world's biggest wind turbines. The one on the right has blades that measure nearly 1 kilometre across.

Wind farming

The biggest wind turbine can make enough electricity to supply a small town. To make electricity for a larger area, a wind farm is needed. This is where a number of smaller turbines are built close together.

These new wind turbines are being tested out on a wind farm in California, USA.

These are Darrieus turbines. They work no matter what direction the wind is blowing.

Wind farms have been set up in many countries but there are more in California, USA, than anywhere else. As well as making electricity, new designs for wind turbines from all over the world are tested here.

A wind farm must be in just the right place. Coasts, high plains or mountain passes are all places where the wind blows for most of the time.

When a good site is found, scientists measure the wind speed and direction and work out how many turbines to build.

This drawing shows Britain's first wind farm at Capel Cynon in Wales.

Work began on the windmill farm in 1988. It is in a windy place on high ground and near to the coast.

People living near this wind farm in California say it is very noisy.

Wind farms cost a lot to build but they make electricity cheaply. They do not use fuel or harm the environment.

However, wind farms can only be built in the windiest parts of the world and they take up a lot of land.

This wind farm is on the coast of Denmark.
It makes electricity for 600 homes.

One idea is to build wind farms out at sea
where it is nearly always windy. But this would
cost more than building them on land because
the turbines would need to be stronger.

This diagram shows how extra wind energy is used to pump water uphill. When electricity is needed, the water is let out through a water turbine.

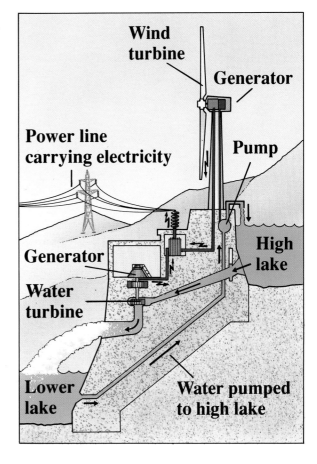

On some days the wind blows harder and this makes more electricity. Extra electricity can be stored in large batteries or used to power a water turbine.

In the future

Many people believe that wind energy will be an important source of power in the future.

Many countries in the world are planning to build wind farms. People are also starting to use the wind's energy to make power in other ways.

This modern Japanese ship is powered by the wind as well as by ordinary fuel.

This machine uses the energy of the wind and heat from the Sun to make electricity to work a powerful light.

This is a new kind of wind turbine. As designs get better, more countries are starting to use wind turbines to make electricity.

Make a wind turbine

Make this wind turbine and see if you can trap the energy of the wind!

You need
a pencil and ruler, a square of thin card 30 cm x 30 cm, a 30 cm piece coat-hanger wire, the empty casing from a ball-point pen, two washing-up bottle tops, a drawing pin, three corks, string, sticky tape, glue.

Use the drawings to help you.

1 With the pencil and ruler, draw two lines from corner to corner across the card.

2 Make pin holes near each corner and in the centre where the lines cross.

3 Cut along the lines about halfway towards the centre.

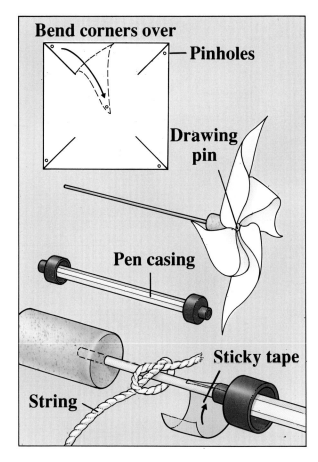

4 Bend over the corners with the pin holes into the centre. Make sure all five holes line up. Push through the drawing pin.

5 Use the drawing pin and glue to fix the windmill on to the cork.

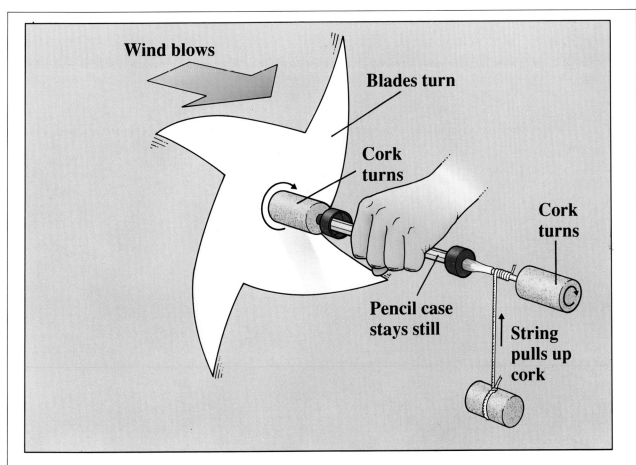

Wind blows

Blades turn

Cork turns

Cork turns

Pencil case stays still

String pulls up cork

6 Push the coat-hanger wire into the other end of the cork.

7 Slide a bottle-top along the spindle up to the cork. Slide on the pen case. Slide on the second bottle-top up to the pen case. Use sticky tape to keep it in place.

8 Next to this, tie a piece of string. Put sticky tape over the knot so it won't slip.

9 Push a cork on to the end of the wire.

The diagram shows you how to use your wind turbine. Tie a cork, or other light object, to the string. Hold the wind turbine very straight and point it into the wind. The blades should turn, spinning the wire spindle and winding up the string to lift the cork.

Glossary

Anemometer A machine that measures the speed of the wind.

Batteries Containers which have special chemicals in them which produce electricity.

Clipper An old-fashioned, fast sailing ship.

Environment The world around us - the air, water, land, plants and animals.

Fossil fuels Fuels such as coal, oil and gas found deep under the ground. They are formed from the remains of plants and animals that died millions of years ago.

Generator An engine powered by a turbine that makes electricity.

High plains Flat areas of high ground.

Horizontal axis turbines Wind turbines which have blades fixed on to a lengthways pole, or axis. The wind makes the blades spin around the axis.

Hurricanes Very strong, swirling winds that blow at more than 118 kilometres an hour (kph).

Megawatt One million watts. A watt is a measure of electricity.

Mountain passes Passages, or gaps, through mountains.

Pollution Poisonous waste, such as the harmful gases

and chemicals that are given off when fossil fuels are burned.

Post mill A windmill built round a central post so that it can be turned to face the wind.

Tower mill A windmill where the top part (where the sails are attached) can be turned to face the wind.

Turbines Machines that are turned by the kinetic (moving) energy in wind or water.

Vertical axis turbines Wind turbines which have blades fixed on to an upright pole, or axis. The wind makes the blades spin around the axis.

Water turbine A turbine powered by moving water.

Books to read

Electricity by Graham Peacock (Wayland, 1992)

Fun with Science: Air by Brenda Walpole (Kingfisher, 1987)

My Science Book of Electricity by Neil Ardley (Dorling Kindersley, 1991)

My Science Book of Energy by Neil Ardley (Dorling Kindersley, 1992)

Where does Electricity Come From? by Susan Mayes (Usborne, 1989)

Windy Weather by Jillian Powell (Wayland, 1992)

Index